In Green Pastures

Poems Inspired by God

Karen J Chisholm

In Green Pastures

Poems Inspired by God

Karen J Chisholm

Inks and Bindings
888-290-5218
www.inksandbindings.com
orders@inksandbindings.com

Books by Karen J Chisholm

I AM with You
Poems Inspired by God

Tough as Nails
Poems Inspired by God

Voices
Poems Inspired by God

This book is dedicated

to the Glory of God

and

My sons:

Joe G. Harker III
Jay M. Harker
Justin M. Harker

I am so proud of you
and so thankful to God for all of you.

Table of Contents

Treasure!

Author

Preface

Many servants have I. Each has dedicated their life to My service. They minister to those I give them and their titles, their job descriptions, are multiple, as are their blessings now and their reward in heaven.

Each, every, any, whosoever serving Me by serving others is doubly blessed whether or not they are thanked. These are the ones willing to be unnoticed, unknown, unseen as they carry out the work I have equipped them for and given them to do. These are Mine.

What they do brings Me souls who want to know the God these people so obviously love and deeply believe in.

Child, you are one of My servants. You take time to sit and write for Me. You wait in silence and scribe what comes to you, unknowing whether these are My thoughts or your own, but compelled to capture them all.

And when the writing is done, you see it is Me speaking through you, thus coloring My words with your brush.

What you do not see as clearly is that I have imbued your very being, your thoughts, words, and actions with My Presence. Thus you are dyed with the Holy. You are the color of praise, of joy, of humility and kindness and peace, of Me. The fruit of the Spirit drips off you onto others wherever you are. In truth, your vessel overflows.

Tell here what I have given you to tell.

Father

Jump!

In Green Pastures

Plenty and generous
Tasty and fine
Easy to get to, so
Just come and dine!

All is prepared and
Is ready for you
Height of the season
And fresh from the dew.

Come while the sun shines
Yes, come while you may
Long before husbandman
Turns it to hay.

Feast on the riches of
Nutrients there
Eat until satisfied
Dine without care.

Here are green pastures
Grown righteous and true
Planned for the care of
My loved ones like you.

This is the book I have
Written o'er time
Wealth of My People,
All those I call Mine.

History, yes, but
Oh, so much more
Wisdom and training
And truth laid in store

Waiting for those who
Will come to find Me
Promise and consequence
For all to see.

Here you learn mastery
When you've long plumbed
Testament to testament
Leads to My Son.

Clear revelation of
God's perfect plan
Laid from foundation
Redemption of man.

And not man alone
Indeed, the whole Earth
In setting of galaxies
Gem of great worth.

Read here and know Me
Prove what you've heard
Here in green pastures
Called My Holy Word.

Adore Me

Come to Me for all.
Seek Me,
Look for me,
Adore Me.

You have never seen
What I can do
Through one
Who adores Me:

Inhabit your praises,
Find truth that breaks all yokes,
Quench sin's fire,
Open blind eyes,
Cause deafness to flee.
You have never seen,
You cannot imagine.

Begin to fathom,
Begin to adore Me.
See what I can do,
See My Spirit move.
Spend all your words,
Exhaust all your groans,
Give your body to be burned,
Let My fire consume you,
And you will finally have room
In your heart for Me . . .
And I will move in.

Deeper, truer, greater, bigger.
Examine yourself.
How much do you want Me?

How much will you give?
Will you give all?
Will you let go?
May I truly have you?

To have, to hold,
To love, to fill,
To use for My glory?

And I get *Great* Glory.

Then adore Me.
Begin to Adore Me.
Come,
Adore,
Come.

Good Morning!

Good morning, child!
It's a bright new day for you.
My mercies this morning are new.

Fresh mercy for the day.
Fresh manna comes your way.
New words I want to say.
Good morning!

All around, sparkling light
Washing away dark of night
Flooding your soul,
Making it bright.
Good morning!

Beautiful song 'round you swirled,
Joyous singing unfurled,
Spreading o'er your tiny world.
Good morning!

New truths uncovered, revealed,
My Word no longer concealed,
By Spirit opened with zeal,
Good Morning!

Come early, stay late.
All hunger to sate,
My Word on your plate,
Good morning!

Joy, gladness, strength for today
Gospel-shod feet on the way
Go forth; and My Words you'll say
God morning!

You'll feel me with you, too,
All of this lovely day through.
I AM your portion new
Good morning!

Have a nice day. ☺

Child, You Love Me

Child, you love Me.
Willing to go the extra mile.
Willing to serve Me, willing to touch Me,
Willing to obey Me.
While others serve the ones they love
Or boss or self or need, you wait.
In My presence, taking time for Me,
You love Me, child.

Child, you please Me.
Willing to write. Willing to wait.
Willing to come. Willing to expect.
Too many expect and run from it,
Shunning the responsibility that comes
To do what I ask.
You please Me, child.

Child, you trust Me.
Willing to do whatever I say.
Willing to listen, to go, to stay.
Waiting, writing every word I say
And trusting what you write is true.
You trust me, child.

Child, you want Me.
Willing to give all that you are.
Willing to trade time for Presence.
Willing to buy without money.
Willing to eat hidden manna.
Laying aside concern and pride,
Rather have nothing and sit at My side.
You want Me, child.

There is NOTHING I won't do for you, child.
Ask and I will give it.
Remain at rest with deep soul peace.
For I AM . . . in you.

Forever Be with Me

I guide your footsteps and decisions,
In every word, let be found Truth.
Follow Me without derision,
Live in Me without reproof

For you are Mine.

You are Mine. I AM your own.
Live in My Love, be not dismayed.
Be found in Me -- in Me alone.
I bear you up, your price I've paid.

You are forever Mine.

None by thee have I loved so well,
Beloved joy and great sunshine.
With Me I see you're pleased to dwell,
For I AM yours and you are Mine.

In Me you dwell.

Accepted sacrifice you are,
Great joy and peace I've given you.
My own alone to use in love
Surrendered self, you've given too

To reach the lost.

To draw them to Myself, My Life,
To save their souls, to set them free.
To show them mercy, end their strife,
Once slaves to sin, now born in Me

Their lives My own.

And so, each day together live,
Great praise and worship, all you give
And blessings always follow you
Where e'er you go, in all you do

For you are Mine.

My life poured out, My sacrifice
You understand, though now in part.
Valued now -- your love's My price,
I died for all -- the Father's heart

Let whosoever come.

And I will walk with you this road
And I will hear you when you cry
And I will bear the heaviest load
And then be with you as you die

Forever to be with Me.

.

Unforgotten

It is My Pleasure

Many times as you read My Word,
And meditate thereon,
Spirit plants new seeds within you,
More and more you're drawn.

I have deeper life for you
Than new shirt or new dress.
I reveal deep wisdom, truth.
It's with these I bless.

All that's gone before prepared you.
Trials broke off bands
Of pride and shame, of guilt and blame,
So emptied you would stand

And let Me form you as I would,
A vessel fit for use
To spread My gospel, blessing, love,
Not stay selfish recluse.

Many songs and hymns and rhymes
I've given toward My Plan
But I chose you in Christ alone
Before I made the world or man.

I saw this day when you would sit,
Receive these words, and say,
"I'll do it, Lord, I'll share Your gift
And trust You all the way."

Now opening before you,
Door of opportunity:
A difficult and lonely path
Glorifying Me.

So pack your bag with gifts I give
That you will give away.
I didn't call you as a salesman,
By faith you'll live each day.

Where I provide your sustenance
And in each place you find
Just enough light to reveal
The path I have in mind.

My blessings now await you,
So finish books of rhyme.
Make ready all I've given you
For this appointed time.

You will sing for all who'll listen,
I've prepared each heart.
They will recognize My voice
All you must do is start.

So trust Me as you pull away
From safety ropes you've tied.
Resign your job, let go your life,
You know I'm true and tried.

For now begins your life, your calling,
Now put feet to words.
You will walk the truth you've written.
My voice will be heard.

Go wherever I may lead you.
Take whate'er may come.
Always thank and follow Me.
The journey's now begun.

And the pleasure . . . is Mine.

Joyous Loud Praise

Nothing and none come between you and Me.
Love is your best accolade.
Walking in closeness and joy by My side,
You will see miracles made.

If I should lead you through trial, so what?
Many have walked there before.
There, ground is fertile for blessings unknown,
This life holds much yet in store.

While you're thus walking, I will be with you,
I will be holding your hand.
Miracles, commonplace, pepper those days
In great adventure I've planned.

Your life I'm using to draw men to Me.
Your words will bring life like water
To souls dry and brittle and fainting, brought low.
Manna from heaven, My daughter.

What you have written will buoy many souls,
My word will not return void.
It will accomplish My purpose indeed,
Already launched, well deployed.

I have prepared those who'll carry it on.
Those know My voice, hear Me well.
Many awaiting assurance rejoice
As they read these words that you tell.

Hear Me now, reader, yes, hear with your heart.
I have called you to My side.
I offer hope of salvation and light,

I give you peace deep inside.

Nothing and no one can wrest from My hand
Those by My cross I set free.
Death holds no fear for the ones who are known
Who, wherever they are, worship Me.

Praise that is soft, loud, or grating, I welcome,
Offered from vessels of clay.
Joined with the voices from those gone before,
I welcome Mine every way.

Joyous rejoicing and great jubilation
Offered from hearts where I dwell
Echo in heaven and down through the ages,
Joined with new voices to swell.

None can imagine the force of the sound,
Its greatness, so vast, overwhelms.
In heaven, it's part of the fabric of all
My pavilions, yea, My glory realms.

I welcome singing, no voice is too low,
Or too raspy or off key for Me.
Praises of men cut them lose from distractions.
Truth told, it is worship sets free.

That's the connection between God and mankind,
The bond that grows stronger with use.
Each soul offers worship-filled words,
Souls drenched with joy know the Truth.

And Christ is revealed to each one who so offers.
More Light of Life fills these hearts.
Praise offered freely brings joy to us all.
Cementing our love bonds, it starts.

More often you praise Me, more glory abounds
In your life, in your family's salvation.
Yes, praise is the key to your faith, for it shows
I'm real, I'm alive in creation.

And when you bring worship, you too are creating.
The words from your lips energy!
Your faith is renewed and then grows ever stronger.
You offer yourself shamelessly.

Bonds that have held you from growing in grace
Fall away as you worship, arms raised.
Embarrassed regrets lose their power to hurt
As you blatantly offer your praise.

And that's why I say don't forsake the assembly,
For in corporate worship you find
The stronger you sing, the more blessing you bring
To each other with none left behind.

In my Word there is David
Who danced, laughed, and sang,
Who shouted his praise before all.
Rejoicing abandoned, just glowingly praised
My holiness held him in thrall.

This is the man who is most like My heart,
Fearlessly worshipping Me.
Shouting and leaping, his joy overflowed,
His spirit danced, gloriously free.

Give Me less careful, soft songs that sound holy.
I long for your joy to flow free.
I like big, loud cymbals and drums that resound
With loud voices that glorify Me.

There's energy there that will free you from sin,
Connection in Spirit affirm,
Bring health to your marrow and joy to your soul
And free you from feeling a worm.

I too rejoice when you sing, dance, and shout.
I join you and My Spirit soars.
Among you, within you, going in and out
And filling your right to your core!

The windows of heaven flung open before you,
My glory cloud covers it all.
I'll give anything for a soul who will bring
Me this glorious praise and stand tall.

Do not let the doubters, the proper and staid,
Lay their bounds on the way you may praise.
Let them keep their aplomb while you enter in song
To My *joy* and to Me your voice raise.

And now you are seeing I yearn over you
Because there is praise in you hidden.
I want your free worship -- I dwell in such love.
In excitement and joy, praise is bidden.

Come to Me often and shout out your joy
In the life I have given to you.
Bondage will flee; you're empowered to tell
Others how to find their freedom too!

So tell!
    Just yell!

Some say, "Why yell? God's not deaf.
He can hear the smallest of whispers unsaid."
Others say, "God is not nervous either."
Though right, here's better way instead.

Each from his own soul will offer Me praise
In the way I have made them to do.
But one will get answers beyond their petition
When they offer praise that breaks through.

Will you . . . break through?
Then praise!

Life is a Melody

Come to Me.
Just come to Me.
I will receive you as you are.

Every moment you are Mine.
Every breath, I'm there.
All you need I have supplied,
Rest in Me; let go all care.

Every, only, one I've made
Gives Me pleasure, fits My plan.
Some for this, some for that,
Every woman, child, and man.

You have your place in this grand scheme,
All of life's a melody.
Everyone you interact with
Harmonizes you with Me.

When you meet one and you "click"
There's a complementing song.
Others you meet, you say, "Ick!"
Because the harmony's all wrong.

Fortunately, I'm directing
Buoyant melody or grim.
Every harmony perfecting,
It's My plan, it's not My whim.

Value, then, the souls I've placed there
Close to you, you close to them.
Every word and interaction

Leads to glory and Amen.
It's peace and joy when you're in Me.
I'm directing, writing new,
Life is song, it's harmony,
Arranging voices, flat with true.

Giving you what needs to be
Removing some, in time you see.
As in music, same, then change.
Unfamiliar, rearrange.

Then repeating what's before,
Second ending. Wait! There's more!
Soon I have my symphony.
All parts work together, see?

Every life a different song
Concerto, Cha Cha, fugue,
Relationship with Me unique,
Cut time or rhythm crude.

All you see and know, I use
My timing's never late.
In your life-long song to Me,
I AM God, I orchestrate.

Because Life . . .
	is a melody.

My Delight

You are My great delight and pleasure.
There is none who can compare.
You are My beloved one and treasure.
You are the fairest of the fair.

And My longing is toward you.
There is none else can take your place
I draw you near; you love Me too.
For I have loved you face to face.

You came from darkness into life.
And I'll not let you go again,
You are My own and My delight.
My Joy, My Love, come enter in.

I Am taking you with Me
Into the future I have laid,
Into far places you can't see.
My plans for you cannot be stayed,

I know the plans I have for you,
Delight you in Myself, I will,
To bring you good, to show you truth,
And you will love Me deeper still.

And I'll not stay my hand of trial
In your vessel that I'm molding,
For you'll need toughness in your vial,
Precious treasure I AM holding.

To present complete to Father
When this life's lived like no other.
And you come
For you . . . are Mine . . . My delight!

My Supply

Child, you are mine. You need only ask.
Yet worry impedes; you falter with care.
I meet every need You have for each task.
Take no thought for tomorrow, for I'm with you there.

If you are short of that which you need,
Blessings abound that cannot be measured.
You've merely to ask and I'll intercede.
Your worth above rubies, you are My Treasure.

Keep your eyes on Me, not darkness that smothers.
Trust I'll provide -- you're not sure in what ways.
This light affliction will fall with the others.
Don't fall for the trap the enemy lays.

Keep coming; keep trusting when you're in a bind.
You know you can trust -- by My eye, you are led.
All things considered, child, you're doing fine.
Despite how you feel, offer worship instead.

One thing makes a difference in what you perceive:
You always feel better, feel filled when you've sung,
Praise and deep worship can set spirit free.
So worship in trial and see it undone.

Believe what I've told you, come trust Me some more.
I've plans you don't see yet that haven't come through.
You'll have what you need on the day, not before.
Just know you will laugh and rejoice when they do.

I know what you need and it isn't a stone.
So stand, pray, and worship while I hold your hand.
Deepest need is relation to Christ -- Risen One.
He stretches your faith and builds up inner man,

Today you are all right, you have what you need.
What you must have I supply for each task.
You've even enough to give others seed.
Remember I'm with you, you need only ask.

And I will supply . . .
  Every time . . .
    You ask.

Not Finished Yet

Nothing Pleases Me More

You have time for Me.
You take time to sing praise.
You remember My statutes, My Word.
You dedicate time in My Presence,
Humbly seeking My face.
Opening My Word, you write out the verses
So their meaning can soak into you.

And nothing pleases Me more.

In choir practice, you remind all
To think on the words and to worship.
Your everyday language is full of My praise
And thanksgiving just stays on your lips.
When plans have been made but are blocked,
You are calm, looking for good to come through.
Steady, you serve Me -- humbly, you help.

And nothing pleases Me more.

You arise early to spend time with Me.
Hunger, un-dreaded, cannot claim your mind.
Patient in sorrow, humble in trial,
You bring all to Me, in My Name.
Every day brings its own ways.
You've learned the days are a gift from My hand.
New mercies each morning you praise.

And nothing pleases Me more.

Nothing pleases me more than your love.
Your thanks keep you so close to Me.
You see trial coming on nation you love
You want a free nation and people without idols
You ask humbly for Me to draw
Souls to the kingdom, salvation for mankind,
Those you love from the brink of hell's maw.

And nothing pleases Me more.

You serve openhanded who crosses your path.
This frail earthen vessel I use for My purpose
You adore Me, delight to be learning My ways.
You come every morn to the well.
To draw out salvation and share it with all,
Asking for souls to be added each day
Before to the world they succumb.

And nothing pleases Me more.

Service – Love

To serve,
Truly, selflessly serve,
There must be love.

Gratitude does not last
For there is a time
When gratitude is at an end
And self is reasserted.

Love never ends.
Not even death
Can bring an end to love.

Gratitude is payment, Love is a gift.
In gratitude,
Service seems almost like homage.
Love is homage.

Do you love Me?
Your love is completed in service.
All the little things you do to please Me
Spring out of love.

You never tire of thinking about Me.
You give up your own pursuits
In favor of time with Me,
Never viewing it as time wasted.

You want to hear the thoughts
Of your loved ones
And you cherish their words,
Remember their voices.

Do you love Me like that?
Or do you write My words
Just to see how many you can collect?
Do you serve Me?
Or do you love Me?

The call of God now asks:
Do you love Me?
The measure of your love is service.

How much do you love Me?
The measure of your service is love.

Who is first?
Me?
Your special friend?
Yourself?

Will you leave all to follow Me
If I ask it of you?
Do you love Me?

Share My Love,
Share My Word,
Feed My sheep.

Serve Me . . .
  And I will see . . .
    Your love.

Dance in My Love

Difficult times, decisions so hard,
Multiple voices opine.
Do the right thing, stand on the Word.
I Am with you, child, you're Mine.

Afterward look back, regret what you did,
Ask My forgiveness and trust.
Loved ones supported, yet still others judged.
You look to the One who is just.

Not born to be hermit, you give away smiles.
I made you to glorify Me.
Alone in My arms, you rehearse others' words,
But I see what you cannot see.

You're free!

Your spirit rejoices, you dance in My Love!
You twirl and your spirit takes wing!
Nothing represses your worship above,
All heaven glows when you sing!

Anointed by God to sing praise, spirit soars!
The chains of regret fall away!
Freely you offer the joy I've outpoured.
My Glory shines as you sway.

Your hands lifted up are like torches of light.
My enemies around you are scattered.
Strength from above comes by grace as you sing,
And all forms of bondage are shattered.

That's why I tell you to sing every day:
Nothing can touch you, cause pain.
While you are worshipping Abba alone,
You're filled up with joy once again.

My joy flows freely from wells of salvation,
Strengthening you to go on.
Singing My Word is like sharpening your sword.
It slices clean when it's drawn.

Bringing good news and delivering hope,
Causing the sly one to flee.
Growing in grace, truth brings more praise
To lips dedicated to Me.

Sing on through your trials,
Pray long and then stand.
Each time you are wounded, seek Me.
Remember the sacrifice, scars in My hands.
I paid your sins' debt, you're free!

To dance . . .
  In joy . . .
    For Me.

Aware

I AM available to seekers.
You are one who has followed
And I AM a rewarder
Of those who diligently seek Me.

Child, you are Mine.
In you I reveal
Mysteries of heaven
Charlatans would steal.

You have no agenda,
Are waiting here for Me.
You will follow closely.
I will let you see.

Mysteries long hidden:
You will write them plain.
Spirit comes unbidden,
Surprising you again.

You have noticed small things
Texture, fragrance, wind.
Little things unhidden,
You see God within.

I AM surging power:
Only energy.
You are led by Spirit
He's revealing Me . . .

To you . . .
  Who are . . .
    Aware.

Growing in Grace

I have put My vision before you.
You have embraced the vision.
You have answered My call
With a resounding, "Here I am, use me!"

You have committed to pray,
To be trained as a warrior in prayer.
You have been told briefly
To expect change.

You see the ministry you are now doing
Lines up with the vision,
And you are encouraged,
Knowing you are on the right path.

Do you know—do you KNOW
That I love you?
That you want what I want
Pleases you, pleases Me.

My vision is bigger than you can foresee,
But you are all in nonetheless.

Know now that I love you,
Your willingness, your enthusiasm, your joy
Because you are in My presence.

I hear that as a baby's giggle.
I see it as a promise of what is to come.
Only know that the vision is in its infancy.

I see it fully mature and know
What I intend to do through you.
But I am enjoying this time of infancy with you.
I am enjoying, too, the euphoria you feel
Knowing you are in the center of My will.

Remember as you grow
To assess what stage you are in:
Walking the floor at night
With a demanding baby
Unexplained sickness
Hungry for more! Now!

Tantrums
"I do it myself"
The terrible twos
Fear of strangers, of change
The trusting threes
And so on.

Lean into Me in the tough times.
Rejoice with Me in the day you see
The blossoms on the tree,
Knowing that fruit will follow.

Labor with Me to get rid of the weeds,
The pests, and the little foxes.

Examine your own heart
And see whether your attitude
Is hampering My vision.

For remember:
Every little thing you do -- or don't do
Has eternal consequences
For someone.

Be a good soldier. Slog through the mud.
Root out the anger, wrath, bitterness,
And deal with it directly.

That is, bring it to Me
Immediately . . .
In prayer.

You are not "tattling," saying
"Johnny won't play nice."
You are recognizing the enemy's devices.

You don't know
How extremely important
This truly is.
Yet.

Now, go have a nice day.
We have not yet begun the hard part.
Giggle some more.

Appreciating

Praise is an Attitude

Praise without words is still worship.
It is your sacrifice of time to be with Me.
It is laying aside your thoughts of you,
What you want. and what you don't want,
And focusing on Me in worship.

It is being thankful -- Eucharisteo.
It is running to Me in trouble, resting in Me.
It is choosing not to fear the future.
It is accepting trials and challenges

Rehearse My works in your life.
Talk about your love for Me.
Tell people how I have blessed you.
Tell what I have brought you through.

Be open and transparent
And ask Me for big things when you pray,
For when I answer those prayers,
All who learn of what I've done grow in faith
And open themselves to Me.
They want to know Me too,
And I AM pleased.

Come, let Me feed you with hidden manna,
Opening conduits for blessings to follow,
And always expect good to come in time.

Focus on Me.
  Think of Who I Am.
    Prayer is a sacrifice and
      Praise is an attitude.
        Get an attitude!

Just Humble

You come to Me humbly, yet not knowing how,
You worry not humbled enough.
I laugh as I hold you and whirl you about,
For I know just where you get this stuff.

Don't you know coming and offering Me praise
Is all of the humbling required?
I take you, your offering, just as you are.
You come because you are inspired.

Spirit within you has brought you to Me,
Given you breath to say all you will say.
You are expressing what you feel inside.
I hear you perfectly, draw you this way.

Lay every fear aside, let the praise start!
Once you begin to praise, I fill your mouth.
It's not your words that count, I hear your heart.
With groanings and laughter and tears that come out.

Out of your spirit, out from inside,
Out in your actions, and I take great pride
In all that you offer Me because you come.
In coming, I fill you with praises begun.

And I joy right over you, I take your praise
And use it to raise you with My Holy ways.
Child, I rejoice and I fill up your heart
With Love from the Father to offer in part.

You take what is given and make it your own
And offer it freely, and each time you've grown.
You're closer to Me and it's easier to come,
All burdens lain down as you laugh with the Son.

Your load has been lifted, your spirit just flies
And you know so much better your Father all wise.
Because you are offering praise to the Son,
Your spirit is dancing for you've become One!

With me,
Holy Three,
And you're humble.

No stumble,
Just humble.

Today

This is the day I have made
I gifted you to know it.
I graced you with experiences
To see how I would show it.

Everything I bring to sight
And every sound you hear
Are brought to you by senses five:
See, touch, taste, feel, hear.

Not equal gifts, yours nonetheless,
These are the tools of life.
And with them you learn every day:
Child, pet, husband, wife.

There is another sense some know
That only is awakened
When you are saved, some say converted.
Then your world is shaken.

This is when I come to dwell
With you in your heart.
Here's where faith begins to grow,
It's where new life must start.

Today is offered every sunrise,
Mercies new each morning.
All are bid to know the Savior,
Invite may come with warning.

Because today is all you have,
Tomorrow is a curtain.
Abundant grace draws every soul
Each sinner wanted, certain.

And every soul makes their own choice
While life may go awry.
Then, when they come, I don't think twice,
I welcome them on high.

Because of Grace,
Because of Mercy,
Because of Love
Today.

Knowing

Keeping commandments won't bring you life,
I AM the Truth and the Way.
Only relationship brings the new birth
Led by the Spirit each day.

Mercies anew every morning are yours,
Grace every moment you'll find.
Open your heart, your will, and your life.
Die to yourself in your mind.

Search for Me daily and watch for Me too.
Focus your thoughts upon Me.
Read, meditate, and remember My Word.
When you find Me, your mind will be free.

And I'll take you up and supply every need
For your name's written here on My hand.
If you come as a child does with nothing but trust,
You will joyously embrace My plan.

I will comfort you close and you'll know My face
When you seek me with all of your heart.
Then you will know My amazing grace
And that's when your questions will start.

You're already loved with My everlasting love.
All you need do is say yes.
You will find more than you ever imagined
As I lead and guide, your life bless.

It's knowing Me that brings peace to your life
And My grace that lifts every care.
It's My pen that writes happy ending to strife
And My life with others you'll share.

Take It!

Receive all I have promised you.
Believe it is yours.
Take action to show
You believe those things you have asked for
Are in your possession already.

Walk out your faith.
Prove Me.
Die to self, to fear,
And receive what I have promised you.
Take it now.

Put your hands on it in the spirit
And bring it into reality.
If I speak to you in the imperative
For you to take action,
You believe as you do.

You receive what you ask for
By taking hold of it.
As in Heaven, so in Earth.

When you say, "Hand me that pencil, would you?" And
know the person near you heard,
You hold out your hand in expectation
And the pencil is put in your hand.

You must do the same thing in the spirit.
When you ask me to give you anything --
New shoes, food, or to open your mind
To thoroughly understand the scriptures,
Take action!

Do what you would do
If you could physically see Me
Holding out My hand
With what you asked for in My hand.
Take it!

And please remember
To use your manners
And say thank you.

Wait.. What?

The Moment

Focus here on Me.
This is My minute in your busy day.
This is what I ask of you
That you walk My way.

Focus clearly on Me now,
Search for Me inside.
Find Me in the silence,
I AM at your side.

Closer than your breath,
I draw your thoughts to Me.
Words of praise fill your mouth
When with spirit see.

I anoint your senses as
You open to receive.
Here, where heaven touches Earth,
Now, while you believe.

And for a moment out of time
I take you in the spirit
Revealing things you never knew,
You sense much more than hear it.

And with the feel of awe and wonder
You take in Old Truth
With new perspective, revelation,
Timelessness of youth.

No such thing as age in spirit,
Judgment here suspended.
All respected, valued, welcomed.
Here no knowledge ended.

Father's Love extends to all
Who grew some and then fell some.
Blood of Jesus ends The Fall
And unbelievers welcome.

History is put aside,
Experience is now.
Where blood-bought sinners now abide,
It's not just who, but how.

And then the moment passes,
Looking 'round, it's same old place.
But there's a difference in you now
For you've beheld God's face.

And now you see and recognize
He's in those you meet.
His Spirit in you reaches out
Fearless, in Him complete.

An interesting thing you note:
Seems love has replaced fear.
And peace remains within you now,
You sense His Presence near.

In time, you may forget this day
But changed you'll always be.
You know My Spirit's with you now
For you belong to Me.

Here in this moment,
    You are
        My Beloved.

In Your Trial

Come to Me in your trial
The moments you spend in My Presence
May be the only respite you have.
Ask Me, not to end your suffering,
But to fill you with My strength to endure.

When you focus your attention on Me,
Only for a moment,
You break the stronghold of this world.
In this moment, the comfort of heaven is yours.
All that I AM is poured out on you
And you surface from your pain
Long enough to receive My strength
To go on, to endure.
In this moment, My Peace is yours
And *why* is not a factor.

Come to Me often.
Speak My Name.
I am here, in this moment.
You become aware of Me,
Knowing I AM with you.

And that alone is enough.

My Little Sheep

Daughter One, you are a seeker.
You keep on coming to your Source.
You want to know Me deeper.

The trials of this life, the storms
Oft brought you to your knees.
Yet you held on by rope of faith,
Anchored here in Me.

And still you seek in quiet time
To hear My still, small voice.
My word took root in you for sure
The day you made your choice.

The seed was planted long before
By pictures in Sunday school,
And you remember making sheep
From cotton glued to spool.

Pipe cleaner legs encircled wood.
Each child's sheep looked so different.
You brought yours home triumphantly
To show off to your parents.

And through the years you heard the Word,
Receiving it with joy.
Though every Sunday guilt was heaped,
Repentance you'd employ.

Your heart was open and you learned
My grace unknowingly.
And when time came life overwhelmed,
You knew to call to Me.

Through every trial and wrong, delay
You wondered when you'd learn.
But I could see you here with Me.
I knew you well. You'd turn.

And every time you'd run away,
You still talked just to Me.
Even rebelled a time or two.
You thought of how you'd flee.

But you never did.

You'd tied yourself to the altar
By repenting at age 10.
And though it tried, you'd not abide
In this world's enticing sin.

Eventually you gave your heart,
Surrendering your life.
Acknowledging what I foreknew,
Your soul belonged to Christ.

Now long years since, you've served Me well.
You bring Me constant joy.
And when you pray, the enemy
Shudders and runs. Attaboy!

It won't be long until the day
You see Me as I AM.
And when you come, look like the Son,
Another spotless lamb.

Destiny

Plans are good, yet incomplete
Until you lay them at My feet.
For all your work, yes, all your plans
Won't buy you time in life for man.

My Word tells true when it declares
The days of man are numbered there
In book I keep, I only know
It's there the final numbers show.

And each one lives, fulfills his days,
Lives out her life in human ways,
And each one lives life path I laid
Because I know how each is made.

In heaven there is no surprise
Come to my ears, before My eyes
For I know all; I made each one.
I see each life before begun.

I know which man will wed which bride,
I see their wants, I know their pride.
I love each one, I see each choice,
I know their frame, I hear each voice.

My Love for all comes to each one
And each decides about My Son.
I give the rain, the sun, the moon,
I tell them all I'm coming soon.

Yet each life matters, deployed by Me.
I yearn over those I've made, you see.
My love for mankind, deep and sure,
Remains forever whole and pure.

So, whosoever makes the choice
To serve Me: those who've heard My voice,
Are welcomed, wanted, wooed, and led
To find Me, hear Me in their head.

They'll know Me, for to them I seal,
And show Myself, My Power reveal.
Their faith built solid on My word
Brings prayers as though
Through megaphone heard.

Direct line, as it were, you see,
I know them, each one who serves Me.
I keep them: never lost a one.
Each hid in Christ, My only Son.

Each living soul may come to Me.
I welcome those who would be free.
Don't judge the ones who will decline,
Just thoroughly love those I call Mine.

I call . . .
And each will hear.

Their answer . . .
Is their destiny.

I Still AM

Amazing.
If nothing goes right and all is lost
But you still breathe,
I AM.

If your sure thing turns out to be
A gamble you wouldn't have chosen
If you'd known,
I AM.

If you were perfectly happy
Driving your old car and had a year to go
Until you could buy a new one
But its usable life was cut short,
I still AM.

If sickness came into your life
And the sit-ups you've vowed
Were halted by a pulled muscle,
You're still My Own.

If your plan to help another
Turned to burden unexpected,
I'm still here.
I've got you.

If the world turns upside down
And all you know is changed,
If the news you heard this morning
Means life as you know it all is lame,

If the trials that you go through
Are so complete nothing remains,
You've got Me.
I AM.

Great I AM.

You can trust Me in each footfall,
I AM with you on life path.
It may be hard to the point of death,
Yet even there
I carry you.

Be sure I know what fiery trial
Has got you bound.
You see, I AM with you in that fire.

In your freedom, in your bonds,
In the dark and light of life,
I AM with you.
Always with you, never leave you.

Trust Me.
I AM trustworthy.

You may never know this side of Glory
Why you were chosen for this.
But I know.
And I AM with you.

Keep on walking
And remember . . .

I still AM.

Silly with Joy

Eternal

Child, you are Mine.
Learn what it means to be a child of Father-God.
Learn that you are loved with an everlasting love.
I do not grow old; no, I AM ever the same,
Yet My mercies are new every morning.
My Grace that you walk in is beyond measuring
And has no boundaries, no beginning or end,
And flows to you, around, over, and through you
Without stopping.

My Blessings are upon those I call Mine
Even before they are aware of Me.
Before they love me, I know them
And see them as they will be.
I love them – and you – with a Love
That cannot be measured, cannot be contained,
Cannot run out or ever stop.

I AM Love. I AM from everlasting.
I have always existed. I never end,
And that means you will never end either.
Your form will change, but you were created
As an eternal being and you will always exist
With or without form.
Your consciousness will never end,
You will always be aware,
For you are made in My image.

Tell me what your thoughts are
On the subject of being eternal.

Lord, I am stretching my thoughts to You.
I am an eternal being.
I have always existed and will never end.
I dwell as a spirit within the body issued to me
When I was born into the family You chose for me.
When this temporary body grows old and expires,
I will have a new body that will never grow old.

And I have a Savior, Jesus, the Christ.
When I see Him in heaven, I shall be like Him.
He is the first fruit and I am a fruit also.
Your family is growing, Father God.
I know You are pleased with Your Plan for mankind,
And I am pleased with You.

I do not truly comprehend all You are conveying,
But I believe it to be true.
I cannot explain it because I do not have words
For much of it.
I am like a young child trying to speak
Of things too wonderful for me.
So I simply stay open to Your Spirit,
Awaiting Your good pleasure,
Serving and loving You,
And serving and loving others like me
Who know You and love You.

I am here, Lord, seeking You who are Eternal.

Seeking God, Learning Truth

Don't jump up when the song is done,
The poem ended you'd begun.
Keep sitting still with pen in hand
And keep on writing 'til I'm done.

More I've brought you, led you to
Each day's treasure something new
Ever, only loving you . . . in Christ.

Think of Me, of where I dwell
Both in your heart and heaven as well
I transcend time, I'm everywhere . . . yet in you.

Stop and look inside yourself
There where I AM, where your heart swells
Center on Me, the One who saves you . . . for Me.

I delight in leading you
Out of danger, into truth,
Closer still inside Myself,
Nearer daily, share My wealth . . . with you.

For through you I can touch more lives.
The more you learn and My Word thrives,
The more I give to share with all.
Lay down your pride, answer My call
To share . . . Me.

Today's the day I've brought you to
Today's the day I'll see you through
My Presence stays, My Spirit hovers
New truth you find, mysteries uncover,
And tell.

And if your understanding's small,
It will grow the more you call
On Me and spend our time in prayer
Waiting . . . waiting.

I will lead you into truth,
Not all at once, but what I choose.
And if you're judged, say honestly,
"I'm learning . . . I'm learning."

Trust is key to keep on track
Expecting answers, ignoring lack,
Investing time and energy in Me.
You'll see . . . eventually . . . the Truth.

And every second spent to find
The One you love who's more than kind
Will change you 'till you look like Me:
Forgiving . . . forgiving.

So you'll not judge another's walk
You'll understand that by their talk
They're searching . . . for something.

And you will tell of joy you've found,
Of Lord you love, find common ground
Agree . . . with Me . . . I'm love.

And now, you may go into your day, Love,
Seeking God.
Learning Truth.

Just Praise Me

Child, the most important thing
you will need to do today
is love Me as I love you
with no reservation, no doubt,
no holding back, and no embarrassment.
I know you and I love you deeply, truly, freely.

My death on the cross
Trumps every faux pas *every time*.
Open your mouth and talk of Me.
What better use of your tongue is there?

Tell of what you know: I AM faithful.
Sing to me any way you want
And I will gladly hear you.
Open your mouth and give Me praise.
Wave your flag and lift your arms,
Lift your voice so others hear your thoughts.

Smile, yes, but more than that, *laugh!*
Laughter with Me breaks ALL bondage.
Don't give me that wan little smile,
You open yourself and give me full belly laughs!
Don't short change My blessing!

Do I have to pry praise out of you?
Don't give me meek, barely heard
Words of praise.
I want to hear you shout words of praise!

Shake off propriety.
Strangle self-doubt.
Throw down this worthless meekness
And SING!

Get out your book of songs
And lift your voice to ME!
Do it!
Sing!

Joyous, loud praise works miracles,
Cleanses you, resets your focus,
And makes you wholly aware of Me.
The best thing you can do *any day*
is to offer Me praise.
It solidly connects you to Me
It pleases me,
And with it, you bring Me glory.

Child, just praise Me.

Anew

Holiness I shunned,
In guilt I hid in shame.
So great this dread I could not rid
Until the Savior came.

When the burden grew
Too great to bear,
A friend led me
In sinner's prayer:

Jesus, I don't know you well.
I'm ashamed and cannot tell
All the bad things said and done
In darkness to God's Holy Son.

My shame, regret grow heavy,
And if a price You levy,
I cannot pay the cost here,
Cannot take back one shed tear.

There is no one to carry,
No reason one should tarry,
To help a worthless sinner
Who'll never be a winner.

But I have heard of You now.
You welcome sinners somehow.
The guilty ones You cherish,
Deliver the nightmarish.

Love for sin You've traded
For many low, degraded.
You bore the sin for all men.

Your blood atoned, like life mend.

To every soul who seeks you,
Repents and turns from sin too,
You offered your life for them:
Redeemed the souls of all men.

Now any who accept You
Are born again and made new.
You set our life clock over,
An offer that will sober.

It's not another chance, it's
A brand new life that each fits.
And none can do it so wrong
Your Grace exhausts. It's that strong.

I want to be one who wins.
I want to be born again.
You offer here to buy my life.
It's not worth much with sin rife.

I accept offer of grace,
Offered hope of no sin trace.
The sale is made; my soul's bought
With burden, guilt, regret stocked.

And I am filled with light here!
Washed clean, brand new, shed thank tears.
The darkness gone! How's that so?
Too good to be true, I'll trow.

But no! It's real! You're with me!
Live right inside and I'm free!
A miracle of new birth
Brings awe and joy of true mirth!

How do you do that, buy lives?
What do with old where sin thrives?
Desires are gone that dragged me.
I'm not sure how to live free.

So You will send me Teacher
And I will hear the preacher
And it will be all good news.
Now that's something I can use!

This new life's working for me.
All's new, each flower, rock tree.
My eyes see beauty, peace store.
Your love surrounds me, heart soars!

I'll never miss the old days.
I'm living now in new ways.
I'm thankful for You, Jesus.
You've bought me; now I can trust.

Made anew,
Thank You.
New me,
I'm free.

Faith Walking

Focus. Focus. Focus on You.
Keeping Your Word on my lips.
Smiling, calm, walking in truth,
Believing my foot cannot slip.

Over and over returning to trust
Remembering . . . just to breathe,
Living, moving in You as I must,
Allowing myself just to be.

I cannot make one hair white or black
By thinking it into existence.
Likewise, no worry will fill up my lack.
Trust alone battles resistance.

This day will happen with me or not,
While I'm here, I must engage.
Worry removes my mind from this spot
And keeps me too long at this stage.

I would go higher and farther in faith
On hind's feet of faith and belief.
You've got my problems covered by grace.
I can rejoice in relief.

Laughing and dancing, rejoicing and free,
I choose to thank, not to plan.
You have it covered; You watch over me.
Joyously, I hold Your hand

And trust
   which is faith
      walking.

Giggles

Mirror, Mirror

I work hard to be right.
"You can do anything
If you want to bad enough,"
The mantra I have said.

But my hard work
Brings such small gain.
'Stead of getting there,
Seems farther ahead.

I see Your Word, I hear You say,
"Be transformed, be made new."
So I do my best to keep the path,
Though fall back, I look to You.

Little children learn to walk
By stepping out, then falling.
They get up and go again,
Keep trying, even bawling.

When their daddy takes their hand
With steadiness, direction,
They go farther, faster with
Encouraging words' inflection.

Pick me up, Lord, dust me off,
And set my feet back on the path.
I'll hold Your hand and lean on You,
You'll keep me from all wrath.

I'll eat Your Word to know you more,
My Necessary Bread.
And when I look for You in there
I'll be transformed, Paul said.

Mirror, mirror, Word of God,
Reach to You, I do.
Leaning harder on the Lord,
Strength to strength renew.

When I see me as Your Word says:
Righteousness of Christ,
Hid in God with You, I'm changed,
Look different deep inside.

New perspective,
Changed direction,
Better goals,
Less imperfection.

Mirror, Mirror, Word of God,
Be my sustenance.
As I gaze into the Truth,
Give me more Your luminance.

Trials yet come, but I am looking
High above the storm
Resting on Your sure, kept promise
I am safe and warm.

Mirror, Mirror, draw me to Him,
Let the Word change me.
When I look to see myself,
It's Jesus looking back at me.

Jesus Knows

Many times, I am worn,
Shocked with grief, lost and torn.
Jesus knows; He's here, I see.
He hears, He cares, He sets me free.

Holy, Holy, Three-in-One,
I lift you up, God-Spirit-Son.
I run to you, in You I hide,
Lord of all, my spirit guide.

I magnify You, keep You close
Lord, I love You, with no boast.
Father, Father, Lord of mine
Precious Jesus, strengthening Vine

Thank you, Lord, for loving me,
For dying on that cruel tree.
Lord, I give myself to you.
I'm yours to guide; I'm yours to use.

Jesus . . .
    You know . . .

Grasshoppers

Though many, the same,
None with a name,
Soldiers of God many times.
Uniform bodies, all colored alike, move,
At God's bidding, they climb.

They hop and they chew,
Destroy all they go through
As they move through the land on command.
And when they are gone,
Time reveals with the dawn,
That men grieve for the famine at hand.

But size is the thing,
Though the numbers are high,
For a grasshopper's not very big.
When the spies bring reports
Of the land back to tell,
Different perspective, graves dig.

Looking through God's eyes,
There's nothing too hard.
God gave us glasses of faith.
So we could see too
As we then look through
And see God's perspective of grace.

Amazing! Miraculous!
Everything possible!
Nothing too hard, out of reach.
Through Christ, by faith,
We know we can do!
Grasshopper faith to the breach!

And how many of us
Does it really take
To make a big difference for one?
When we join in prayer,
And we know God is there,
Us grasshoppers get the job done.

My Hope

Hope connects me to You, Lord.
Hope isn't seen, but is real.
When trials come and my world is undone,
Hope has become my soul seal.

Hope becomes faith over time.
I find I can trust You to stay.
I'm living Your Word, each promise I've heard,
I rest in this hope day by day.

Then, when trials come with great loss,
I'm blinded by grief; I am numb.
You carry me through; I cling only to You,
I wait and watch You overcome.

My hope is a strand in the cord
That keeps me connected to You
With faith intertwined and Love, the God kind,
I'm still standing when each trial's through.

And when sun comes up each day,
You are what's right with my world.
You've always stayed
Through the messes I made.
Surprised, I find my tears hope-pearled!

This hope is what's left in the end.
It's where I live when I am old.
When You come for me,
Blessed Hope I too see,
We will walk hand-in-hand on streets gold.

What can I say?
You are My Hope, Jesus

Keeping the Rules

Lord, am I doing Your will? Am I working for God?
Am I loving, forgiving, no blame?
Am I careful for others? Am I selfish still?
Keep remembering just why You came?

Or am I stubborn, must have my own way,
Defending my rights and ambition?
Obstinate, others must heed things I say,
Speak for You, hide my sinful condition?

Whenever I'm pleased that I get what I want,
I'm grieving the Spirit inside.
You said meek and humble and gentle in heart.
When it's me first, I'm living in pride.

Your Spirit, Lord Jesus, devolves to me grace.
My purpose in Earth: pass it on.
Oneness with Father, time seeking His face
Will dissolve selfish pride as I'm drawn.

You told me, Die daily, yea minute by minute,
Dead to self: nothing to lose.
No one offends by word, deed one who's gone,
So to die to self daily, I choose.

You have a few rules like keeping the Sabbath.
You offer Your blessing for all.
To be born again from above, in the spirit,
To honestly answer your call.

And then, as we're born, we start dying to self.
You live in us, Jesus; we're new.
All hardships that follow removing the dross,

By Your Word we're to do what You do.

Insisting our own rights denies You deliver,
Denies Christ within, meek and lowly.
We persecute You when we build ourselves up.
Stubborn self-will stabs The Holy.

If we'd be disciples, true followers of Christ,
We would follow our perfect example
To be one with God, only speak what He says,
Be Ignored, cheated, lied to, yea trampled.

But begin, then continue, to love like the Father
This is our reasonable service.
If we're dead, won't display our own temper this way.
If alive in Christ, none can unnerve us.

So, in keeping the rules that were laid down by Christ,
What we owe to mankind, simply love.
When robbed, we give love, when we're hurt, do the same,
Doing will of the Father above.

What's in it for us? Deep soul satisfaction
And freedom we've yet to explore.
Taking His yoke on our necks with the Son,
We'll own less, but gain so much more.

Am I keeping the rules? Am I dying to self?
Every day do I come, checking in?
Am I hiding Your Word in my heart 'gainst the flesh?
Am I in for the long term to win?

You said, Take My yoke upon you and learn
I AM meek, lowly, and gentle in heart,
And you will find rest for your souls, you'll find Me.
And I answered, Here I am, Lord; let's start.

Treasure!

Servant's Heart

A servant does not complain
But carries out the work,
Reserves all observations,
The difficult does not shirk.

Endeavors unobserved,
With right heart does each task,
Is truly valued by none
Until this life is past.

And God sees.

All will come to light,
Each deed and look and motive.
Real servant from the heart
Revealed as true devotive.

Plain is seen the false,
The selfish who have stolen
Honor due to those they serve
While own importance swollen.

And God knows.

So while we are now serving,
Let us keep hearts pure
By serving Christ as we serve others
His glory to assure.

Trust the Lord to make our way
His way, His purpose, plan
And offer our deep conscience clear
When last day take His hand.

And God is pleased with His servants.

Secretly

Has anyone ever told you
How to spend your money?
Everyone has the answer
And thinks one should have plenty.

Say, "If you knew what I know,
You'd do the same as I.
And you'd have lots to show for,
Just give it a try!"

But they don't walk in your shoes.
They don't see things your way.
And your concerns don't touch them,
So they don't get a say.

Your heavenly Father knows you,
Sees the desires of your heart.
And sometimes He will lead to
One of those He's set apart.

You see, your Father watches
Those others do not see.
And He provides for sparrows
And people who are not free.

He has all of the cattle
Upon a thousand hills,
So monetary blessings
To generous hands he fills.

And tells us it's a secret
When we give unto the poor.
Wants it done so quietly
Few know when we give more.

You see, He would protect them
From judging eyes, more pain,
Embarrassment and worthlessness
When kudos givers gain.

Take care to not do good deeds
In public before man.
In humbleness and quiet,
Slip money in a hand.

And while you're at it, share a smile.
Pass on the Father's Love.
It's just a moment here below
Recorded up above.

And all the times you've shared like this
With open hand for other
Secretly with little flair,
You've done it for a brother.

And you've performed a servant role
For Father up in Heaven.
You've been His hands and feet below
Each time that you have given . . .

Secretly.

The Shepherd

The ninety and nine
Who were left behind
Were doing what they were told.
The one who was lost
Roamed at his cost
And couldn't get back to the fold.

The shepherd was grieved,
A little bit peeved,
But looked 'til he found the one lost.
For this wayward sheep
He would lose sleep,
Hoped 't'would not be to his cost.

A story you say
Told by Jesus that day
Who would know as he'd been with the shepherd.
When David slew lion
Had strength without tryin'
Just a kid, one who knew God had heard.

And Jesus Himself knew
'Bout keeping his sheep few,
Told Father he'd not lost a one.
Except for Iscariot,
One who would bury it,
The man who'd betrayed God's own Son.

So who gets the Glory
When telling the story,
Redemption for one out of many?
The Father of Light
Who only is right
Will seek out the lost one, yes, any.

Whoever will come
Stands redeemed by the Son
Any time they cry out, call his name.
From their seat in a chair
Or the maw of a bear
For salvation is never a game.

Life?
Or Death?

All you need . . .
  Is to talk . . .
    To the Shepherd.

Look!

Every complaint or caress you may share,
Every sweet word, sigh, or cluck
Reveals your thoughts clearly, like radio blare.
See? I'm with you when you get stuck.

Look up! Remember that I'm always here.
Loving, no matter delay.
Come as you are and bring Me your fear.
I'll give you grace for today.

Come open, honest, and bring Me your pain.
Bring Me your sin and regret.
I'll make a trade; you will sing new refrain.
Come early and see what you'll get.

Peace for each moment to carry inside,
Grace to have mercy on self,
Glory eternal to share in, abide,
Enjoyment of fun things for self.

Every tomorrow extends from today.
Choose only good thoughts to share.
Remember it is I Who am leading the way.
Hand over each trouble and care.

Let's take the path that is longer but fun:
I've things to show on the way.
Know you can trust Me for I've made you Mine.
I'll teach you to value delay.

Life just goes better when I hold your hand.
I help you over the hard spots.
You'll come to trust Me when life turns to sand.
I help through all life's hard knocks.

I'll sing over you. Look at what I have made:
There's beauty to find all around.
The roar of the river, and quiet of glade,
Fresh impartation each sound.

Look at life better when you're close to Me.
Self set aside, you do fine.
Let's walk together and I'll help you see
All of the Glory that's Mine.

Oh, look!

With Thankfulness

I worship You, am thankful too.
You give me words I feel inside
To offer up with heart of love,
Forgiving, letting go of my pride.

And following more closely still
Your scriptures tried and true,
Each day I walk close by Your side
More focused here on You.

Irritations come thick and fast,
Sometimes my temper flares.
If I can keep my big mouth shut,
You handle it with grace to spare.

Then, when the major woes of life
Block out the sun inside,
I find a reservoir of hope,
A peace that yet abides.

And that is what I cling to when
My life is torn and swept.
I find that peace, center in You,
Gain strength to take another step.

Journey then continues on,
You carry me sometimes
Until I'm ready, have to face
This different life, this harder climb.

Keep looking back to better times,
Forgetting what's before.
Don't want to learn to live again,
My heart bereft and sore.

But patiently you lead me on.
What can I do but follow?
With tears my bread, I hold Your hand,
Walk, though inside I'm hollow.

You lead me gently to green pastures.
Others come and sit beside.
Bring me strength with words unspoken,
Sharing grief locked deep inside.

Make me eat when I forget,
Reminding me to shave,
And slowly, inexplicably,
Joy comes in unexpected ways.

The darkness passes and I find
My eyes behold new things.
And I begin to laugh again.
My heart once more can sing!

And I appreciate my life
In ways not there before.
I'm calmer now, restlessness gone,
Each day's a treasure store.

I look for You in tiny things.
New patience I employ.
I speak to others, taking time
To really hear them, share their joy.

And as I look inside myself,
I'm seeing good things come.
Stop finding fault, accepting now
The work in me You've done.

I worship You with deeper love.
I long to see Your face.
In ways I never knew before,
Appreciate Your grace.

Don't let me forget, return
To selfish life I lived before.
Remind me in the quiet hour
Only You are Lord.

"Lest I forget Gethsemane,
Lest I forget thine agony,
Lest I forget thy love for me,
Lead Me to Calvary."

With thankfulness . . .

Amen

Author

About the Author

Hello, I'm Karen J Chisholm and I live in a suburb of Houston Texas. It has been my pleasure to share with you the things Jesus says to me in my morning time with Him, and a few of my own thoughts as well.

God absolutely loves us. He *is* love and Glory.
I encourage you to make yourself available to Him. Spend time with Him in prayer and when you are through talking, just listen. Soon you will realize the words coming to you are personal, like He is reading your mail. If you are like me, you will want to grab a pen and paper and write those words down to think about later.

God bless you!